Introduction

My name is One-eyed Willy. I live in a cozy home in Huntington Beach with my two brothers, Titan and King Tut. The three of us love each other and are always playing. And guess what? I only have one eye, but that is a story for another chapter.

Dedication

This book is dedicated to Sherry Montgomery, the founder of A Home 4 Ever Rescue in Costa Mesa, California. Sherry's heart is ten times the size of a normal person's, and her unwavering dedication to saving as many dogs as she can is inspiring. Her compassion and commitment serve as a beacon of hope for countless animals in need.

A Home 4 Ever Rescue operates entirely with the help of volunteers and is a 501(c)(3) charity. We rely on the generosity of kind-hearted individuals to continue our mission of rescuing dogs. It is through the selfless efforts of people like Sherry and the support of our community that we are able to make a difference in the lives of these wonderful creatures.

I also extend my deepest gratitude to Greenleaf Publishers LLC, who have not only encouraged and supported me throughout the creation of this book but are also responsible for bringing it to publication. Their belief in my work has been invaluable, and I am profoundly thankful for their partnership.

To all who have contributed to this journey, I thank you from the bottom of my heart. Your dedication, support, and generosity have made this book possible.

Acknowledgement

I would like to extend my heartfelt gratitude to Michael, whose humor and creativity brought joy and inspiration into my life. His delightful impersonations of my dogs and his imaginative take on what they might say if they could talk never failed to make me laugh.
Michael's encouragement and support were instrumental in my journey to complete this book.

Throughout the process of writing and refining the stories of One-Eye-Willy, Michael's belief in my ability and his valuable life lessons kept me motivated. His insistence that I never give up on sharing these tales has left an indelible mark on this project. Although we have since parted ways, his influence and the laughter we shared continue to resonate with me and have played a crucial role in the completion of this book.

Michael, your presence may no longer be a part of my daily life, but your impact remains. Thank you for being a source of inspiration and for helping me bring this book to life.

We have the best Mom ever! She works in the city at a law company and sometimes clients come to our house. But her main job is being an awesome mom. She makes sure we always have food, cozy beds, and fun toys. We go to the park every other day, and I love riding in the car with the window open, even though Mom doesn't always like it. Sometimes, we stop at the toy store on the way home because my brother Titan always breaks his toys. But Mom still manages to take care of everything and be a super mom!

Titan and I are like twins, almost the same age. We love exploring, playing, and sharing our feelings. King Tut is older, and he acts all grown-up. Sometimes, he tells us off for being too noisy or playful, but we know he loves us and protects us.

I only have one eye that works, but it's okay. I still have fun with my friends, even if I can't see perfectly. Once, we went to the park with Mom, but the weather turned stormy. I got really scared of the thunder and rain. I hid under the car until Mom told me it was safe. She always knows how to make things better.

DOG

Back home, Titan and King Tut wanted to know why I got so scared. King Tut talked about how bad memories can feel like ghosts haunting us until we face them. It made sense to me.

At dinner, I felt like I needed to talk about my bad memory. Titan and King Tut listened, and they promised to help me feel better.

King Tut asked, "What do you mean, Willy?"

"I felt like something bad was going to happen, but I couldn't explain it," I replied, feeling unsure.

Titan said, "We're here to help, Willy. You can tell us anything."

With their support, I shared the story of how I got my name and found my forever home. They listened quietly, and I felt relieved knowing they cared about me.

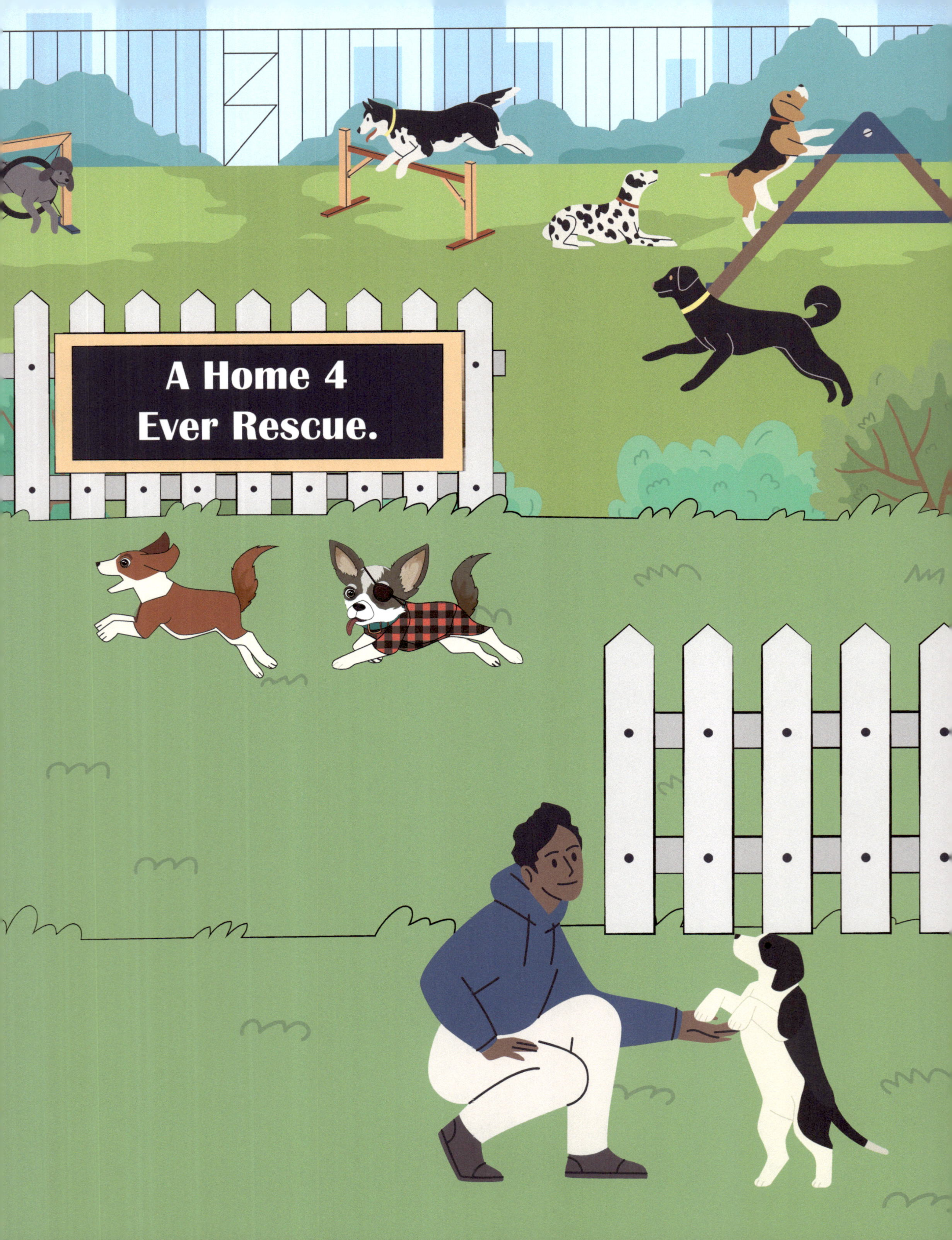

A Home 4
Ever Rescue.

Chapter 1: The Past Life

The Hope Shelter is where my story starts, just outside of Santa Ana. I had a different mother and siblings back then. I had a brother named Buster and a sister named Lily. Buster was a lot like Titan. I was a little younger than him.

All day, Buster was able to keep up with my energy. We were so full of life that people called us the shelter's "dynamic pair." We would plan games and other fun things to do to make the otherwise tough situation more fun.

Lily liked being with our Mom most of the time. At the shelter, we played on our homemade playground all day. Our Mom visited us often, making us feel safe. We became close, having fun together every day, running around and playing games. As time went on, more kids came to the shelter, making it livelier.

One day, while Buster and I were playing. Mom called us for dinner. We were super hungry and excited for a yummy meal. During lunch, Mom and Lily went into another room. When they came back, Lily didn't follow Mom, which worried me. Mom told me that Lily went to her "Forever home" to play with a new family who would love and care for her. I didn't understand what that meant. I asked Buster, but he just said. "You'll know soon."

I missed Lily a lot after she left. Playing with Buster was still fun, but something felt sad without her. Mom worked hard to take care of us and find families for other kids in the shelter. I realized Lily leaving wasn't goodbye; it was a chance for her to have a happy life with a new family. I hope she'd come back one day with stories about her adventures. The idea of a "forever home" sounded exciting, and I look forward to Lily coming back to us someday.

ADOPT
a
PET

Willy
Buster

Lily never came back, and I still missed her a lot. One evening, I sat in the corner feeling sad, and Buster came over with his ball. He tried to comfort me, saying, "Lily found a family who needed her, just like Mom found me and brought me to the shelter." I was confused, so Buster told me a story.

He said, "Mom found me when I was very young near the city and brought me to the shelter. At first, I was shy, but Mom took care of me." He explained that shelters like ours help people temporarily and find them families who can give them a good life. Just like Lily did, I might also find a family and leave the shelter one day. Buster's words made me feel better, and I realized that leaving the shelter could be a good thing. With hope in my heart, I looked forward to finding my own "forever home" someday.

ADOPT a PET
Willy

After a few weeks, Buster also found a new home and was adopted. Before he left for good, he ran to me and asked me to take care of his toys. "I don't know, Buster. I want to go with you so we can play forever," I said. But Buster assured me, saying I would find a home in Santa Ana just like he did. His words stuck with me, giving me hope to find my own forever home.

When Buster left, I felt sad but also excited about the chance of finding a family. The shelter felt quieter without his happy barks, but we remembered him through the toys he left behind. I made sure to take care of his toys and pass them on to new friends, keeping his memory alive.

Mom worked hard to find homes for us, and I was hopeful but nervous every day. When a kind family visited, I hoped they would be my forever family. But when they didn't choose me, I felt disappointed and alone. Days passed without a family picking me, and I started doubting myself. Why am I not good enough for a Forever Home?

Chapter 2: Santa Ana

After Buster left, everything at the shelter felt quiet. Mom stopped trying hard to find me a family. My hope started to go away, but I didn't want to give up. I believed my forever home was still waiting for me out there. Every day, the shelter seemed emptier, and Mom looked worried. So, one night, I decided to go on an adventure. I sneaked out of the shelter when it got dark. The city smelled different, and its lights were so bright! Santa Ana was full of tall buildings, and the night sky looked like a colorful painting. I felt like I could do anything!

As I walked through the city streets, I saw people running past me, their faces filled with worry. I tried to ask for help, but they just shooed me away, saying they were too busy. "Hey, can you help me find a safe place?" I asked a man, but he just kept rushing by, not even looking at me,

BAKLAVA

The wind started to pick up, and the sky grew dark. Thunder rumbled, and big raindrops started to fall. I felt scared and alone. "Mom!" I called out, but she wasn't there. I needed to find shelter fast.

I spotted a cardboard box by the side of the road. It looked like it might keep me dry, so I crawled inside. But the rain started to seep through, and soon I was getting wet. "This isn't working," I thought to myself.

I saw a car parked nearby and hurried underneath it, hoping it would protect me from the rain. But the water started to drip through the bottom, and I knew I had to keep moving.

Finally, I spotted a covered alleyway up ahead. I ran towards it as fast as I could, trying to escape the rain. When I reached the dry spot under the balcony, I let out a sigh of relief. "I made it," I whispered to myself.

Taco Truck
SNIFF

Chapter 3: The Realities of Life

As I walked down the sidewalk, my stomach rumbled loudly. It was a familiar sound, one that usually meant it was time for dinner at the shelter. But now, I was out here on my own, and I didn't have Mom to feed me. I tried to ignore the hunger, but it kept gnawing at me like a persistent itch I couldn't scratch.

Trash and plastic bags floated by, but there was no sign of food anywhere. Still, I kept walking, hoping that I would find something to eat. Then, suddenly, a new smell filled the air. It was the smell of something delicious cooking, and it made my mouth water.

I followed my nose until I spotted a food cart across the street. It was surrounded by people, but I didn't care. All I could think about was getting something to eat. Without stopping to think, I dashed across the road towards the cart.

But as I got closer, I heard the owner shouting at me to stop. "Don't run!" he yelled, but I didn't listen. I was too hungry to care about what he was saying. I just wanted to eat.

As I continued on my journey, another rumble filled the air, but this time, it wasn't coming from my stomach. It was the sound of thunder, and it made me think of Mom. Whenever it rained back at the shelter, Mom would come into our room to comfort us. Buster and I would huddle under a blanket, but Lily wasn't afraid of the storms. Mom would always say, "One good thing about storms is they never last forever, so don't worry." I never really understood what she meant by that until now.
As I walked, I couldn't shake the feeling that the clouds above were watching me, almost like they were asking why I didn't stop when the food cart owner told me to. I imagined them talking to each other, one cloud angry at the other for not listening to him. It was like they were arguing about me, and it made me feel a little uneasy.
"Oh, by the way, did I ever tell you guys I'm a mixed-breed dog?" I blurted out suddenly, trying to lighten the mood. But Titan and King Tut just stared at me blankly.
"THIS IS NOT IMPORTANT NOW, WILLY!" Titan snapped, his ears perked up in annoyance.
"He's just trying to add some drama to the story," King Tut added, licking his paw casually.
"Okay, okay, I'll get back to the story," I said, feeling a bit embarrassed. "You two seem really interested, though."
"CONTINUE, PLEASE!" Titan urged eagerly, and I couldn't help but wag my tail a little as I settled back down to keep telling my tale.

When I opened my eyes, I found myself surrounded by a sea of people, all bustling around me. Their voices mixed with the honking of cars and the sound of someone shouting in the distance. I felt disoriented, like everything was smaller and harder to see. Trying to move, I realized I couldn't. Pain shot through my body, and I struggled to lift my head. Looking behind me, I saw a bright, shiny wall. And then it hit me—I had been hit by a car.

As I lay there, staring up at the clouds, memories of Mom's comforting words during storms flooded my mind. She would always say that storms don't last forever, and her touch would reassure me that even in chaos, there is peace. But now, lying broken on the ground, I couldn't find that peace. The crowd around me buzzed with noise, some taking pictures while others tried to help. The cook from the food cart was beside me, his eyes filled with worry and sympathy.

I tried to stand, but the pain was too much. Every touch felt like an attack, and I cried out in fear and frustration. Amidst the chaos, a soft voice cut through the noise. "Get out of the way, let me see," the woman said. Her voice sounded familiar, like Mom's, but it wasn't her. She knelt beside me, tending to my wounds with gentle hands.

As she bandaged me up, her calming presence eased my fear. She assured me that everything would be okay, and for a moment, I believed her. When she finished, the crowd dispersed, leaving me alone with this stranger who had come to my aid. Her soft eyes met mine, offering comfort and reassurance. I closed my eyes, feeling safe.

Chapter 4: Intermission

I tell Titan and King Tut, "Now you know why I'm scared of storms. And just in case you were wondering, I hurt my eye in the car accident.

As I stop and walk to my bed, I hear a soft sound with a cloudy tone. "Oh, you didn't finish your story." King Tut nods his head like a child and says, "Yeah, you still haven't told us how you got here."

I smile and say, "You guys wanted to know why I was scared of the storm. Now you know." The rain in Santa Ana took my attention away from me. That comes to mind every time I see or feel a storm up close."

"I know, but you still haven't finished the story," Titan says out loud.

I agree, "You cannot leave us at a cliffhanger like that," King Tut comes next. Their eyes light up when I hold their leash. Then I laugh and say, "I was joking. Yes, I'll tell you the whole story."
It makes both of them smile and wag faster. But Mom rushes in the door.
It's late at night, and she is not happy! She scolds the three for making noise and not being sleepy.
"King Tut! Titan! Willy! It's late! You should be asleep by now!" Mom said.
King Tut and Titan quickly scamper to the side of the bed, pretending to be asleep. I just stare with one eye at Mom, my tail thumping softly against the floor.
Mom can't help but laugh at their antics. She pats each of them gently on the head before moving on to just calling for them and giving them rubs and belly rubs.
"Alright, bedtime, you three," Mom says, her tone softer now. "Time to sleep."
One by one, they all take turns receiving Mom's affection until they eventually settle down and drift off to sleep, cozy and content, forgetting all about the story.

"When will he wake up?"
"He will when he wants to, don't disturb him."
"But I want to hear the rest of the story!"
"Leave him alone now."
Titan and King Tut can't stop talking to each other. I was awake and could hear them even though my eyes were closed. Titan kept telling me that he wanted me to finish the story, while King Tut tried to calm him down by telling him to be patient. "Willy, wake up!" Titan's voice jolted me from my sleep.

I groggily opened my eyes. "Good morning, everyone. How long have you been waiting?"

"You're awake, Willy!" Titan exclaimed, bouncing around.

"Only five minutes," King Tut replied calmly. "We're excited for today!"

I giggled and got out of bed, joining them as we headed to the front yard.

Puddles covered the ground from last night's rain. Titan darted around, splashing in the grass.

Come on, Willy! Join me!" Titan called out excitedly.
But King Tut stopped me. "If you jump too, you'll get tired.
Then you can't finish your story."
We gathered for a meal, and Titan apologized. "I got carried
away."
"No need to say sorry," I reassured him. "Let's take it easy."
"Yeah, we want to hear all of it!" King Tut chimed in eagerly.
I laughed. "Calm down, guys. But what got you so excited?"
"We just want to know what happened after the van took
you!" Titan exclaimed.
"We're all in this together!" King Tut nodded in agreement.
Excitement filled the air as we settled down. I began to tell
them what happened after the crash, and they listened
intently, ready for the journey ahead.

A HOME 4 EVER RESCUE
OPEN

Chapter 5: Controlling Animals

I blinked as I stepped out of the van, the sudden flood of light making me squint. My right eye was covered with a big bandage, making everything look fuzzy and blurry. It felt like a wall between me and the world.

But as my eyes adjusted, I saw where I was. It was a new place, different from the safe places I knew. Instead of feeling cozy, this building had a business vibe. The sign above said, "A Home 4 Ever Rescue."

I remembered hearing about it from my Mom. She talked about it with respect and admiration, saying it was a safe place for dogs in need. She loved how dedicated the staff was.

In Costa Mesa. The name brought back memories. Mom said it was for people who loved dogs and would protect them.

Then I thought about the owner, someone who won Mom's love. She was described as kind-hearted and loving to dogs.

Even though I was lost in this new place, A Home 4 Ever Rescue made me feel safe. Maybe it was the buzz of activity inside or the sunlight coming through the windows. But it wrapped around me like a warm blanket.

When I stepped into the busy rescue event, I couldn't believe how many dogs were there. Big ones, small ones, and fluffy ones. They were all there with their wagging tails and curious eyes. This place was different from the shelter I knew. It felt organized and well-taken-care-of.

There were special chairs for tired people to rest while they visited the dogs. Everywhere I looked, there was careful planning and attention to detail.

A person in a white coat, who said they were a vet, checked me over for injuries from the crash. Thankfully, I wasn't too hurt, just my eye under the patch. The vet said I will be okay after fixing my dislocated jaw.

After that, I was taken to a room where the other dogs lived. The room was full of barking and playing. It reminded me of the fun times I had with Buster back at the shelter. But here, I felt lonely among all these unfamiliar faces.

I found a quiet spot to gather my thoughts. Everything felt overwhelming, and I needed some peace in the middle of the chaos. For now, finding calm was the most important thing.

A HOME 4 EVER RESCUE

Everyone turned to look at the woman when she entered the room. The person who greeted her called her "boss," and she said to call her "Sherry." They talked with respect and warmth. Sherry smiled kindly at the man's jokes and called him "Ms. Boss," showing they were more than just coworkers. When she looked at me, I felt calm and comforted by her kindness. "Hi buddy, welcome to A Home 4 Ever Rescue," Sherry said softly, reaching out to hug me. Her touch was gentle and soothing.

With Sherry around, I felt at home. Her friendly personality made me feel safe and relaxed. As she rubbed my fur, I let go of any fear and stress I had.

Falling asleep in Sherry's arms, I felt a spark of hope for the first time since the accident. Maybe things would be okay after all.

My dogs' tails wagged excitedly as Sherry said her goodbyes, and the man left. Olly, one of them, came up to me with a friendly hand.

A HOME 4 EVER RESCUE

"Hello," I said with a smile, and we started talking. I told Olly about the scary car accident I was in and how it made me scared of the dangers outside the shelter's walls.
Olly asked about my wounds and shared stories of dogs at the rescue event who had been hurt or abandoned. It made me realize how big and scary the outside world could be.
Listening to their stories made me uncomfortable. Everywhere you looked, there was danger, and anyone could be a threat.
But being at A Home 4 Ever Rescue gave me hope. I was surrounded by dogs who had been through tough times but found love and support here.
Reading their stories, I understood something important. We were all survivors, showing the strength of the canine spirit. The volunteers and nurses at the event were like lights in the darkness, giving us hope for a better future.
Looking at my fellow rescues, I knew we could face anything together. We weren't alone.

I couldn't shake off the fear swirling inside me as Olly and I shared stories. The car crash showed how dangerous the outside world could be. But everyone at A Home 4 Ever Rescue was friendly and welcoming.

Each dog had a tough story to tell, but we were connected by hope. We all came here seeking help when we were in trouble. The staff took great care of us, and Sherry's visits made us feel loved and remembered. Her care gave me hope.

As days turned into weeks and months, the routine of the rescue event helped me feel safe and stable. Regular check-ups ensured we were healthy.

But while some of my friends found homes, I was still waiting. Watching them leave made me happy and sad at the same time.

As days passed without adoption, I started feeling disappointed. But I promised myself not to give up hope, knowing my new friends and the staff would always be there for me.

Sherry's attention made me feel safe and warm in a way I'd never felt before. There was a special connection between us that didn't need words. She understood my worries and gave me hope when things seemed bleak.

A HOME 4 EV
ADOP
Willy

Her regular visits brought me happiness and reassurance. With every kind word, she reminded me that she cared about me. Her trust and encouragement gave me strength. "Everything will be okay, bud," she'd say, her tone full of passion and trust. Those words became my guiding light through tough times. Even though my eye was covered with a bandage, Sherry saw my promise and strength. I was thankful to have her in my life. Her kindness inspired me to face each day with courage.

As the adoption event approached, I felt hopeful and excited. Sherry's news about the event near Santa Ana gave me a fresh burst of hope. It was my chance to find my forever home.

Sherry worked hard to get me ready for the big day. I couldn't help but feel happy at the thought of finding my own family, even though a little fear lingered in my chest.

As the sun rose and the day brightened, Sherry carefully placed me in a cage, excitement bubbling inside me. She lifted me up for everyone to see, effortlessly showing her expertise. Then, with a smile, she gave me a new name: "One-eyed Willy." I felt strong and determined with this name, a reminder that I could face anything

A HOME 4 EVER RESCUE
ADOPTION DAY

Throughout the adoption event, Sherry stood by my side, waiting for a kind soul to recognize me. And that's when I met Sonya, my new mother. Sonya had long red hair and a heart of gold. As soon as I saw her, I barked until she came to me. She held me close in her arms, and we quickly became inseparable. Sonya was kind to me and took care of me, knowing that Sherry had many other dogs to look after. I soon learned that Sonya had two other dogs, King Tut and Titan.

At first, I didn't like them both, to be honest. I didn't like anyone who spent time with Sonya and received her attention. But over time, I learned to accept them as my brothers. Sherry noticed how attached I had become to Sonya. Whenever I had to leave Sonya's side and return to Sherry, I would cry myself to sleep. I just wanted to be with Sonya.

During the adoption event, I barked at Sonya and then returned to Sherry, but I couldn't help crying as I longed to be with Sonya. I wanted to be by her side all the time.

Sonya took me everywhere with her, even to work. I would hide in her desk drawers, and if I couldn't see Sonya, I would freak out and cry until I found her. I had abandonment issues, and I was fiercely loyal to Sonya.

Despite my small size, I became part of Sonya's family. I even wore costumes for Halloween, like a pirate parrot perched on her shoulders.

Sonya's son lived with her while in college, and I became his little companion too. But my heart belonged to Sonya, and I never wanted to be far from her.

Sonya officially adopted me, and I became her constant companion, even hiding in her purse when we went out. I was her loyal little dog, always by her side.